Learn How To Package Trades In Your Next Negotiation

How To Develop The Skill Of Assembling Potential Trades In Order To Get The Best Possible Outcome

"Practical, proven techniques that will help you get the best deal possible out of your next negotiation"

Dr. Jim Anderson

Published by:
Blue Elephant Consulting
Tampa, Florida

Copyright © 2014 by Dr. Jim Anderson

All rights reserved. No part of this book may be reproduced of transmitted in any form or by any means, electronic or mechanical, including photocopying, recording or by any information storage and retrieval system without written permission of the publisher, except for inclusion of brief quotations in a review.

Printed in the United States of America

Library of Congress Control Number: 2014951957

ISBN-13: 978-1495347764

ISBN-10: 1495347761

Warning – Disclaimer

The purpose of this book is to educate and entertain. This book does not promise or guarantee that anyone following the ideas, tips, suggestions, techniques or strategies will be successful. The author, publisher and distributor(s) shall have neither liability nor responsibility to anyone with respect to any loss or damage caused, or alleged to be caused, directly or indirectly by the information contained in this book.

Recent Books By The Author

Product Management

- How Product Managers Can Grow Their Career: How Product Managers Can Find And Succeed In The Right Job

- Sales Secrets For Product Managers: Tips & Techniques For Product Managers To Better Understand How To Sell Their Product

- Product Management Secrets: Techniques For Product Managers To Boost Product Sales And Increase Customer Satisfaction

Public Speaking

- How To Become A Better Speaker By Changing How You Speak: Change techniques that will transform a speech into a memorable event

- How To Give A Great Presentation: Presentation techniques that will transform a speech into a memorable event

CIO Skills

- How CIOs Can Solve The Security Puzzle: Tips And Techniques For CIOs To Use In Order To Secure Both Their IT Department And Their Company

- What CIOs Need To Know About Working With Partners: Techniques For CIOs To Use In Order To Be Able To Successfully Work With Partners

IT Manager Skills

- Team Building Strategies For IT Managers: Tips And Techniques That IT Managers Can Use In Order To Develop Productive Teams

- Secrets Of Effective Leadership For IT Managers: Tips And Techniques That IT Managers Can Use In Order To Develop Leadership Skills

Negotiating

- Learn How To Signal In Your Next Negotiation: How To Develop The Skill Of Effective Signaling In A Negotiation In Order To Get The Best Possible Outcome

- Learn The Skill Of Exploring In A Negotiation: How To Develop The Skill Of Exploring What Is Possible In A Negotiation In Order To Reach The Best Possible Deal

Miscellaneous

- Power Distribution Unit (PDU) Secrets: What Everyone Who Works In A Data Center Needs To Know!

- Making The Jump: How To Land Your Dream Job When You Get Out Of College!

Note: See a complete list of books by Dr. Jim Anderson at the back of this book.

Acknowledgements

Any book like this one is the result of years of real-world work experience. In my over 25 years of working for 7 different firms, I have met countless fantastic people and I've been mentored by some truly exceptional ones. Although I've probably forgotten some of the people who made me the person that I am today, here is my attempt to finally give them the recognition that they so truly deserve:

- Thomas P. Anderson
- Art Puett
- Bobbi Marshall
- Bob Boggs

Dr. Jim Anderson

This book is dedicated to my family: Lori, Maddie, Nick, and Ben. None of this would have been possible without their constant love and support.

Thanks for always believing in me and providing me with the strength to always be willing to go out there and be my best for you.

Table Of Contents

GREAT DEALS ARE A RESULT OF THE TRADES THAT WE PACKAGE......8

ABOUT THE AUTHOR 10

CHAPTER 1: SO JUST HOW DO YOU NEGOTIATE WITH PIRATES?......15

CHAPTER 2: REAL DEALS USE REAL MONEY AND SALES NEGOTIATORS NEVER FORGET IT 18

CHAPTER 3: WINNING SALES NEGOTIATIONS: THE PIZZA SECRET 22

CHAPTER 4: WHY WIN-WIN SALES NEGOTIATING NEVER WORKS AND WHAT TO DO ABOUT IT..25

CHAPTER 5: SALES NEGOTIATIONS: HOW DO YOU GET FROM THE MIDDLE TO THE END?..29

CHAPTER 6: USING THE BOGEY TACTIC TO GET YOUR WAY IN A SALES NEGOTIATION 33

CHAPTER 7: WHAT EBAY CAN TEACH A SALES NEGOTIATOR 37

CHAPTER 8: WHY SALES NEGOTIATORS NEED TO WATCH OUT FOR THE GIVE & TAKE 41

CHAPTER 9: SALES NEGOTIATORS KNOW THAT A GOOD BARGAIN CAN CLOSE A DEAL 45

CHAPTER 10: WHY TAKING HOSTAGES DURING A NEGOTIATION IS NEVER A GOOD IDEA 49

CHAPTER 11: TO PREPARE FOR THE FUTURE, YOU NEED TO LEARN TO DELIGHT YOUR CUSTOMER 53

CHAPTER 12: THE SECRET GOAL OF EVERY NEGOTIATION................57

Great Deals Are A Result Of The Trades That We Package

What a great world this would be if only we could sit down at a negotiating table, have both sides make a few concessions and then we'd suddenly have the deal that we were all hoping to be able to reach. Sadly, getting that perfect deal takes a great deal more effort on both sides.

The key to successful negotiating is to realize that the only way to get to the deal that you want is by both sides of the table being willing to make concessions to the other side. However, it's when and how those concessions will be made that will determine if you are going to be able to reach the deal that you want.

All too often in a negotiation, concessions can start to involve the use of so-called "funny money" which is not the same thing as real money. You are going to have to be able to detect when this is happening. Ultimately, it's going to take a good bargain to close the deal that you are working on.

When you are in the middle of a long negotiation, it can be easy to lose your way. How to reach the end of the negotiation may no longer be clear. However, by taking lessons from retailers who negotiate every day like Ebay and using tactics like the bogey you can find your way to the end.

Win-win negotiating has been a popular concept in both literature and in negotiating training in the past few years. The reality of real-world negotiating reveals that this type of negotiating rarely, if ever, seems to yield the results that we both want and need. A different approach is called for.

In order to get the other side of the table to agree to what you are proposing, you are going to have to capture their imagination. In the world of negotiating we call this delighting your customer and knowing how to do it is very powerful.

This book will teach you how to move your next negotiation along to a successful closing. We'll show you how to package and deliver your concessions so that your offer becomes irresistible. Examples of how this is done will be reviewed and the tactics that you'll need in order to make it happen for you will be covered.

For more information on what it takes to be a great negotiator, check out my blog, The Accidental Negotiator, at:

www.TheAccidentalNegotiator.com

Good luck!

- Dr. Jim Anderson

About The Author

I must confess that I never set out to be a negotiator. When I went to school, I studied Computer Science and thought that I'd get a nice job programming and that would be that. Well, at least part of that plan worked out!

My first job was working for Boeing on their F/A-18 fighter jet program. I spent my days programming fighter jet software in assembly language and I loved it. The U.S. government decided to save some money and went looking for other countries to sell this plane to. This put me into an unfamiliar role: I started to negotiate with foreign military officials and I ended up having to participate in the negotiations for large international deals.

Time moved on and so did I. I found myself working for Siemens, the big German telecommunications company. They were making phone switches and selling them to the seven U.S. phone companies. The problem was that the switches were too complicated. When it came time to negotiate a deal with the customer, the sales teams struggled to create an effective negotiating strategy. I was called in to bridge the world between the product functionality and the business impacts as they related to the negotiations.

I've spent over 25 years working as a negotiator for both big companies and startups. This has given me an opportunity to learn what it takes to both plan and execute negotiations of all sizes. When it comes to negotiations, I've pretty much been there, done that.

I now live in Tampa Florida where I spend my time managing my consulting business, Blue Elephant Consulting, teaching college courses at the University of South Florida, and traveling to work with companies like yours to share the knowledge that I have about how to prepare for and execute successful negotiations.

I'm always available to answer questions and I can be reached at:

Dr. Jim Anderson
Blue Elephant Consulting
Email: jim@BlueElephantConsulting.com
Facebook: http://goo.gl/1TVoK
Web: **www.BlueElephantConsulting.com**

"Unforgettable communication skills that will set your ideas free..."

Create An Effective Negotiating Team At Your Company!

Dr. Jim Anderson is available to provide training and coaching on the topics that are the most important to people who have to negotiate: how can my team effectively prepare for and execute a successful negotiation that will get us what we both want and need?

Dr. Anderson believes that in order to both learn and remember what he says, audiences need to laugh. Each one of his speeches is full of fun and humor so that what he says "sticks" with everyone.

Dr. Anderson's Negotiating Training Includes:

1. How to plan for a negotiation: what information do you need and where can you find it?

2. What's the best way to explore how a deal can be created during a negotiation?

3. How can you bring a negotiation to a close without giving in to the other side?

Dr. Jim Anderson works with over 100 customers per year. To invite Dr. Anderson to work with you, contact him at:

Phone: 813-418-6970 or
Email: jim@BlueElephantConsulting.com

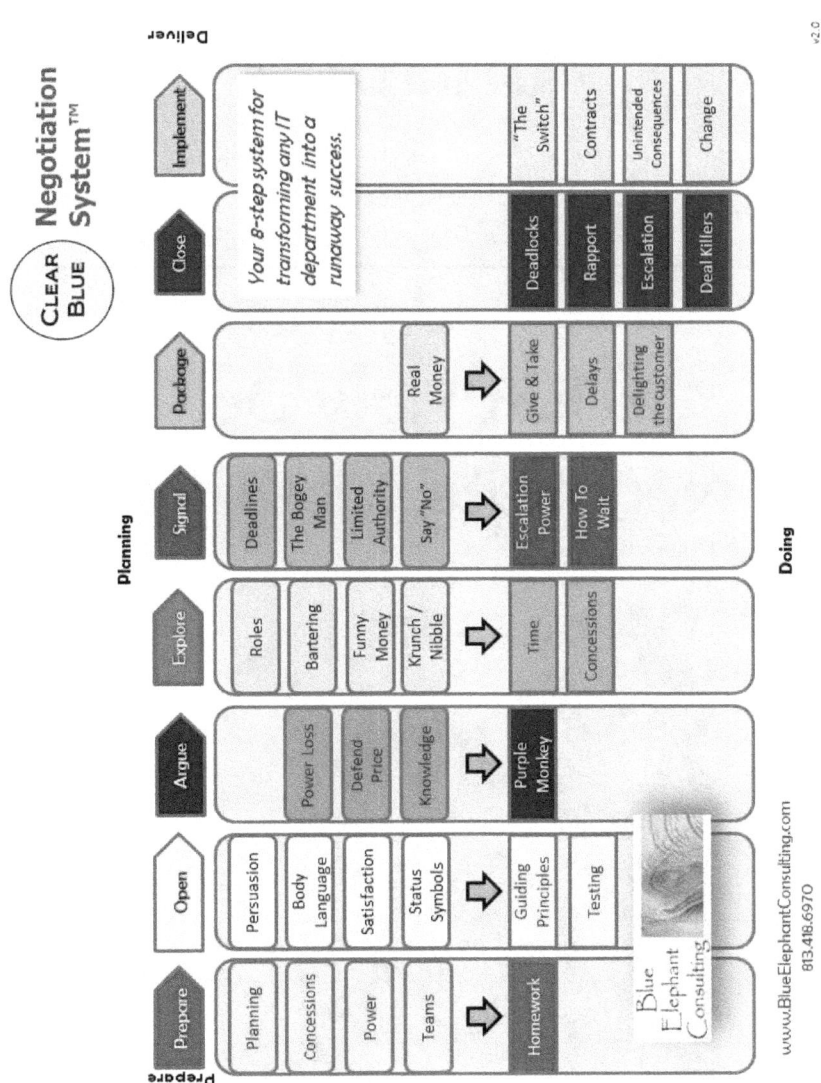

The **Clear Blue Negotiation System™** has been created to provide negotiators with a clear roadmap for how to manage a successful negotiation. This system shows negotiators what needs to be done and in what order to do it.

Chapter 1

So Just How Do You Negotiate with Pirates?

Chapter 1: So Just How Do You Negotiate With Pirates?

Negotiating is both an art and a science. We study what works and what doesn't in order to make sure that the next time that we are in a business situation in which somebody has something that we want; we are able to negotiate to get it. But what about pirates?

The newspapers are all abuzz about the pirates who are operating out of Somalia. So far this year, there have been 96 pirate attacks. Forty of these attacks have resulted in pirates boarding a ship, taking over control, and then demanding a ransom for the ship and its crew. Worldwide there have been 83 reported pirate attacks in the 3rd quarter alone.

When pirates capture a ship, they then demand a ransom in order to release it. These ransom demands are generally in the range of $1 – $2 million dollars. However, in the case of a Saudi oil tanker the ransom may have been as high as $15 million dollars.

What is a ship owner to do if his ship is captured by pirates? Apparently a lot of them are calling Holman Fenwick Willan, a London maritime firm. HFW has 6 lawyers who are currently working on pirate cases. Ashby Jones wrote an article in the Wall Street Journal in which HFW stated that they are working on "over a dozen" of the 20 pirate hijackings that have occurred in the Somalia area.

So just how does one negotiate with pirates? At HFW, their first job after being notified of a pirate highjacking is to calm their customer's fears – nobody seems to know how to react to this sort of thing.

The next step is straight out of the negotiators handbook – do some research. HFW then works to find out just where the hijacked ship was registered, oh, and where exactly the hijacking occurred. This will set boundaries around the negotiations and will determine what laws are in play and will determine who is liable.

The issue of paying a ransom is, of course, a big deal. One key question that the negotiator needs to resolve right off the bat is if it is even legal to pay a ransom. It turns out that under U.K. law, paying a ransom IS legal and that's important because for some reason most marine insurers are located in England.

The actual negotiations with the pirates are, to put it mildly, stressful. The negotiations are conducted by negotiators that HFW obtains for their clients. Forget suits and ties, this special breed of negotiators generally come from the military Special Forces. Probably the right men (I think that I can be sexist here) for the job.

Once a deal has been struck and the ship has been returned to the crew, the negotiations are not over. Indeed, they are often just beginning. The boat owners will now start to negotiate with the firms who were shipping cargo on the boat in order to get them to reimburse them for part of the ransom that was paid. These negotiations can drag on for a very long time.

We are all privileged to live in the 21st Century; however, sometimes aspects of the 1800's, such as pirates, intrude into our world. Thankfully the negotiation skills that have been developed over the centuries serve us just as well now as they did then.

Chapter 2

Real Deals Use Real Money and Sales Negotiators Never Forget It

Chapter 2: Real Deals Use Real Money and Sales Negotiators Never Forget It

My daughter is currently learning about how to add fractions in school. The trick to doing this right is that you have to make sure that the **denominator** (the number on the bottom of the fraction) is the same for both numbers before you add them. She's struggling with this concept and it reminds me of a key sales negotiating point – never try to do a deal using funny money.

Just What Is Funny Money?

We all have heard the phrase "**apples to apples**" right? Well funny money is something that can either sneak into a sales negotiation or be slid into it by one side of the table. When this happens, all of a sudden you aren't comparing two equal things such as how much a product costs and how much you are willing to pay for it. Instead, all of a sudden you've got **apples**, **oranges**, and **bananas** on the table in front of you.

A great example of funny money in real life is what happens when you gamble in a casino: you don't use real money, **you use chips instead**. There are a number of reasons for this, but a key one is that chips don't "seem" like real money. That allows us to gamble more and not feel as bad when they all go away (although it still hurts when we get the bill later on!)

Examples of Funny Money in Sales Negotiations

Whether intentional or not, funny money can slip into just about any sales negotiation. It's the careful negotiator who keeps his / her eyes open and **spots it when it shows up**. Here are a few examples of what funny money can look like:

- **Price per Unit**: If I'm asking you to lower your blue widget price by two cents per unit, that seems like a small matter, right? It is until you realize that I'm trying to buy two million blue widgets and so what I'm really asking for is a $40,000 discount. Now that's real money!

- **Price per Lot**: This is the flip side of the previous tactic. If I'm laying mulch in my yard and you tell me that you'll sell me 10 bags of mulch for $20, which sounds like a fair deal. Until I realize that since I need 200 bags of mulch, we're really talking about me paying you $400 for mulch. The total quantity needed and its price is what we need to negotiate.

- **Interest Rates**: This is exactly what built those credit card companies into the powerhouses that they are today. If I borrow $60,000 at 10% on a 5-year loan to start my business, then I've just agreed to pay the bank $16,489.20 for the privilege of using their money. Sure seems like I should try to negotiate a lower interest rate.

Final Thoughts

It is the job of every sales negotiator to train themselves to always be asking the question: "**what is that worth**?" Just like my daughter who is trying to learn to remember that she always needs to convert the denominator of two fractions to the same value, so too do sales negotiators need to learn to always "**map**" funny money to real values.

No matter what the other side of the table says, always take the time to **translate funny money into real dollars and cents** (or whatever currency you are using). If you don't take the time to do this, you run the risk of making a bigger concession than you intended to. Learn to deal with funny money correctly and this will allow you to close better deals and close them quicker.

Chapter 3

Winning Sales Negotiations: The Secret Pizza

Chapter 3: Winning Sales Negotiations: The Pizza Secret

Recently I was talking with some friends of mine who are planning on using the current depressed real estate market to "trade up" and get a bigger / better house. They were lamenting the fact that this process was going to require them to negotiate with the sellers. They had come to me because they knew that I teach others how to use negotiation to quickly close bigger deals.

What they wanted to do was use that "win-win" technique that they had heard others talking about and they wanted me to teach them how. Sigh. Nothing in life is ever as easy as it seems, but from this experience I thought there were a few key points that you might be interested in...

The Negotiating Pizza

When I started talking with my friends about the house that they wanted to buy, I kicked off the conversation by asking them what they wanted to get out of the negotiations that they knew would be required. They said that price meant everything to them – they could only afford to spend so much money.

Dear reader, clearly we were starting off on the wrong foot. The problem is that my friends were looking at the negotiations for the house that they wanted as a pizza. Assuming that that pizza had been cut into 10 slices, they wanted to make sure that they came out of the negotiations with at least 6 pieces and not 4 pieces. This is not win-win negotiating.

In their quest to get the house that they wanted at the lowest possible price, my friends were approaching the negotiations as a contest – a contest that would have a clear winner and a clear loser. No wonder they were nervous!

A Better Negotiating Pizza

Win-win negotiating has everything to do with how both sides of the table feel after the negotiators are done. If somebody feels as though they've come away with less pizza than the other side, then it wasn't a win-win discussion.

What you need to do is to make the pizza BIGGER. That way it doesn't become a matter of who gets how many pieces, because both sides actually walk away with more pizza.

In working with my house buying friends, I asked them where they had some flexibility – what else could we add to the negotiations besides just price? It turns out that they were flexible on when they could take possession – they didn't need to move in immediately. Also, my friends are handy fixer-uppers and so they were willing to make changes to the house – the current owners didn't have to actually have the work done.

Final Thoughts

In the end, these two additional negotiating points were what allowed my friends to successfully close the deal. The current owners had not yet picked where they wanted to move to so having more time to get out of the house was very important to them. Additionally, they had a lot of fancy furniture that they didn't want to have to worry about covering while the house was being painted, etc. My friends got the house for a fair price and everyone went away with more than enough pizza.

Sales negotiators who learn how to make the pizza bigger for both sides of the table will be able to close better deals and close them quicker.

Chapter 4

Why Win-Win Sales Negotiating Never Works and What to Do About It

Chapter 4: Why Win-Win Sales Negotiating Never Works and What to Do About It

Quick: what's the first thing that you think about when you picture your next negotiation in your mind? Unless you are Mother Teresa's brother / sister I'll bet that you saw yourself walking away from the bargaining table with the best deal in the world, you had gotten everything that you had wanted and more. Umm, what about the other side? That's why win-win negotiating never works.

How Win-Win Negotiating Is Supposed To Work

Too many people have created in their minds a magical world where win-win negotiating (where lions lay down with lambs, money grows on trees, etc.) always works. Instead of worrying about things like price, delivery date, and quantities, you are expected to instead be worrying about how the other side "feels" and what kind of deal will make them "happy". Balderdash.

I don't know about you, but I am forced to live in the real world. Flat out I don't have the time to spend trying to worry about how the other side of the table is feeling today. It may come as no surprise to you that in my experience the other side is not spending any time trying to decode what my lucky mood ring is telling them about my current feelings either.

This kind of Pollyanna approach to negotiating does not work and the folks who go around writing books about it and teaching negotiating courses based on it have created a generation of negotiators who are, dare I say it, ineffective.

Win-Win in the Real World

I like the part about "win-win" where I win in a negotiation; however, I'm a bit leery about the other side winning also, doesn't that mean that I lost something? It sure does if I'm sitting at table with you and a stack of 100 $1 bills and you and I are negotiating about how much of the stack each of us gets. Every $1 bill that you get is one that I don't get, and I want 'em all. I've been in negotiations like this and they are always disappointing.

In the real world you and I are sitting at a table on which there are a pile of eggs, a chicken, and a pig. Now let's start negotiating. Maybe I run a restaurant and you run a grocery store. On the surface things look the same as the stack of $1 bills example. However, this time around we've each got different needs. We actually might be able to find some common ground.

If I'm running a restaurant, then I've got dinners that I've got to cook tonight. If you're running a grocery story then you've got to stock your shelves for this week, we're both trying to solve time related supply issues. Long after the eggs, chicken, and the pig are gone I'll still need to get supplies for my restaurant and you would love to sell those to me.

For creating my dinners, the chicken and the pig are more valuable to me, for stocking shelves for a week; the eggs and the chicken are more valuable to you. I might be willing to give up on the eggs if you'd give up on the pig. In fact when it comes to that pig, I'm interested in using the ham for a dinner and you might be interested in the bacon to go with the eggs that you'll be selling to people buying breakfast food.

What you're seeing here is how our self-interests start to overlap. No Pollyanna "I want to hold your hand" stuff, instead I'm still just thinking about myself; however, as more of my drivers are put on the table we're finding out that you have many of the same drivers. Negotiating a deal that solves more of our common drivers is what's going to create the best long-term solution.

Final Thoughts

Ever since that dang <u>Getting to Yes</u> book came out, negotiators have been pursuing a mythical unicorn-like type of negotiation, one where everyone gets what they want and walks away from the table happy.

In the real world, this just simply doesn't exist. Instead, we find ourselves in a situation where we need to work very hard to make sure that our side of the table's needs are taken care of because nobody else is looking out for us.

Where there is some hope comes from taking a close look at our self-interests and finding out if there is any overlap with the other side's. Where we are able to find common ground, we've got an opportunity to create a deal that will benefit both of us at the same time. As long as I get my chicken and my part of the pig, I'll be happy.

Chapter 5

Sales Negotiations: How Do You Get From the Middle to the End

Chapter 5: Sales Negotiations: How Do You Get From The Middle To The End?

How many times has this happened to you: there you are, you've jumped into a sales negotiation and started off with your initial negotiating position. The other side did exactly the same thing. You are miles apart and it seems like there is no way that you are ever going to bridge the gap. What do you do now?

Movement Is Good

Although it sure can feel mighty lonely when you are in the first half of a sales negotiation, take heart – this is exactly what needs to happen. Both sides always start far apart, have some conflict and stake out their positions. This is when things start to really get interesting.

Expert sales negotiators realize that after all of this posturing is done is when the real work of crafting a deal really beings. Yes, there is a lot of distance between where you and the other side of the table sit right now; however, it's up to you to find ways to narrow that gap.

Your job is to knuckle down and look for which issues you and the other side are closer together on. These are where you can initially spend your time trying to find ways to move closer to an agreement.

Your negotiating strategy and the other side's will be in flux at this time. You'll try different things and some will work, some won't. You will test the other side's commitment to some of their positions and they'll do the same with you.

Much of this stage of the negotiation is based on power. You will be working to find out just exactly what the other side really wants to get out of the negotiation. The goal of this phase is for both sides of the table to come away with the belief that a deal is possible.

Into The Fire

It takes a lot of guts to be a good sales negotiator. You'll have to prove yourself when you move to the next stage of a negotiation – this is when the hard bargaining starts.

Both sides realize that a deal is possible. However, you'll change your tactics. You want to end up with the best deal possible and that means that you need the other side of the table to make as many concessions to you as you can get. Unfortunately the other side of the table is thinking exactly the same thing.

This is where the bare-knuckle brawling really comes out. Different sides threaten to leave, do leave, come back, etc. Pretty much every negotiation tactic in the book gets whipped out and tried during this phase of the negotiation.

This is a very difficult part of the negotiation to make it through. However, professional sales negotiators do make it through by realizing two important things: where they currently are, and where they are close to being. They know that if they can stick with it, they're almost done.

Striking A Deal

You will never be able to negotiate the perfect deal. What will happen is that you'll push and push to get a better deal and eventually you'll hit the brick wall at the end of the tunnel – you're not going to get any more from the other side.

When this happens, you've reached the end of the negotiation. You need to take a moment and assess where you are. Can you live with the deal that is currently on the table?

You need to realize that if you can't, then you are going to have to start negotiations all over with another partner. However, if you can live with the deal, then you are very close to being done.

Assuming that the deal that gets written down accurately reflects what you think that you verbally agreed to (it doesn't always!), then you've successfully negotiated a deal.

What All of This Means for You

Inexperienced sales negotiators can often get lost in the middle of a sales negotiation. They know how to start the negotiation; however, once it's under way and they realize just how much distance there is between their position and the other side's, they don't know what to do next.

The correct thing to do is to realize that you need to spend time working to close the gaps. Once this has been done, you will be in for some hard negotiating in order to move towards closure. A deal isn't done until both sides can agree on a written version of the agreement.

Professional sales negotiators have a secret weapon. They never give up hope no matter how difficult things get. That's what makes the deals that they reach feel so good for both sides of the table.

Chapter 6

Using the Bogey Tactic to Get Your Way in a Sales Negotiation

Chapter 6: Using the Bogey Tactic to Get Your Way in a Sales Negotiation

So there you are in a sales negotiation, you like what is being offered to you but there is one small problem. You don't have enough money to buy it. What can you do? Walking away is of course one option; however, maybe there's something else that you can do. It turns out that this is right time for you to pull out the bogey tactic and give it a try.

The Bogey Tactic

So just exactly what is the bogey tactic? This is when you simply don't have enough money to buy what is being offered to you during a sales negotiation and you tell the other side that.

The beauty of the bogey tactic that, if done correctly, it can turn into a win-win approach to reaching a deal. There's a very good chance that either you've used it in the past or it's been used on you (successfully probably!)

How to Use the Bogey Tactic

When you are in the role of a buyer who is involved in a sales negotiation, the bogey tactic can be your best friend. Here's how you would go about using it.

Let's say the other side of the table has presented you with a proposal. What they are offering is great, but you simply don't have the cash to pay for it. What to do now?

Using the bogey tactic, you'd tell the other side that you like their proposal, but it was currently out of reach of your ability to pay. This would cause two things to happen on the other side of the table. First, they'd be pleased that you are interested in their proposal. Secondly, they would instantly start trying to think of ways that they can still make this deal happen.

You may need to prove your point. This can be done in a bunch of ways. Your goal will be to show to the other side how much money you do have to spend and why additional funds are not available to you.

What You Can't Accomplish Using the Bogey Tactic

If you are trying to get a lower price from the other side, the bogey tactic probably isn't going to help you out. However, what it can do is actually get you more for your money. As the other side works with you to find a way to make the deal happen, more choices will be presented to you to choose from.

Just having more choices doesn't mean that the cost to you is going to decrease. However, by choosing wisely you can end up getting more value for the money that you do end up spending.

Why Sellers Like the Bogey Tactic

Just to be completely fair here, sellers like the bogey tactic also. The reason is because when the buyer uses the bogey tactic, then the seller knows that they are close to making a deal.

There are two things that a seller can do once the bogey tactic starts to be used. First they can test to see if the buyer really is at the limit of the amount of money that they can spend. Often times there are still additional funds that can be tapped and the buyer just needs motivation to find them.

If this turns out to be true, then the next step is to change what is being offered. By substituting less expensive options for what was in the initial proposal while keeping the price at the customer's upper end, the profit margin on the deal can be increased.

What All of This Means for You

All too often during a negotiation you'll be presented with a proposal that meets your needs, but which exceeds your budget. When this happens, you can use the bogey tactic to see if you can move closer to completing a deal.

When you use the bogy tactic, you reveal to the other side of the table that you like the proposal that they are making; however, it's too expensive. This encourages the other side and motivates them to work with you to find ways to lower the price of their offering.

The bogy can work for both the buying and selling sides of the table. The key thing is that by revealing why an offer is too expensive, you may open the door to moving closer to making a deal that works for both sides. Don't fear the bogey!

Chapter 7

What EBay Can Teach a Sales Negotiator

Chapter 7: What EBay Can Teach a Sales Negotiator

Everyone's heard about the web site EBay right? That's where you can go to auction off any junk that you don't want to have lying around your place any more or where you can go to purchase a GI Joe doll that you remember from your childhood (in its original box!). It turns out that the success of EBay holds a number of lessons that sales negotiators should learn from...

Maybe We've Got This Auction Thing Backwards?

When it comes to conducting a sales negotiation, we generally can't run an auction to find the best deal. This just isn't a good way to work out all of the details that go along with striking a good deal.

A much better way of getting a good deal is to use what professional negotiators like to call "a reverse auction". I like to call this technique "shopping around".

What Is A Reverse Auction?

In a traditional auction, what's being bought is presented and then people proceed to bid on it. Everyone gets to see what everyone else is offering. Whoever offers the highest amount of money wins the auction and gets to purchase the item at the highest amount that they stated that they'd be willing to pay.

In a reverse auction, things are run a bit differently. This negotiating technique requires that the buyer approach each potential bidder separately and ask them for a bid. Upon getting an offer from each of them, the buyer now has both a range of prices and a collection of features to choose from.

Things aren't over yet, they are just getting started. Now the buyer can go back to each one of the bidders and state that they can get a better deal from another bidder and ask them if they'd be willing to lower their price / increase what they are offering.

You can see where this is going now. The buyer keeps having separate discussions with each of the potential bidders and telling them what the current lowest offer is. This is done in order to motivate them to lower their offer in order to stay in the game.

Ultimately, the bidders will reach a price point that they are unwilling to go beneath – effectively this is their lowest price. Once this happens, the buyer will need to make a decision about which offer best meets their needs.

The Danger of Using a Reverse Auction

Hopefully you can see just how powerful a reverse auction can be. The bidders have so little information that they end up bidding against themselves in many cases.

However, you can also imagine how a bidder must feel after a reverse auction is over –worn out and potentially angry. Sure they got the deal, but was it a good deal for them to get?

The reason that this matters to you is that if you need to make any changes to the deal that you've reached with the winning bidder, they'll permit the changes, but they'll attempt to reclaim some of their lost profits by increasing their price for the change.

What All of This Means for You

EBay is one of the most successful Internet companies in existence for a very good reason. They provide their customers with an opportunity to participate in auctions for just about every product imaginable. Professional negotiators need to realize just how powerful a technique an auction is, and start to use the reverse auction tactic.

The reverse auction tactic requires the buyer to play bidders off against each other in order to get the lowest price. The danger in doing this is that this may leave the winner angry and wanting to regain lost profits if any changes are needed.

A sales negotiator needs to have many diff

erent tactics that can be used when needed during a sales negotiation. The reverse auction tactic is one of these. Just be careful when you decide to use it – with great power comes great responsibility...

Chapter 8

Why Sales Negotiators Need To Watch Out For the Give & Take

Chapter 8: Why Sales Negotiators Need To Watch Out For the Give & Take

You may or may not realize it, but the other side of the table in a sales negotiation might be as smart, or even smarter, than you are. I say this not to make you worried, but rather to make sure that you remain aware throughout the entire negotiation. A good example of this is the old "give and take" technique – just when you think that you are ahead, you may find yourself way behind all of a sudden …

The Give And Take Technique

The give and take technique of negotiating is very simple on the surface. In fact, when it's being used, the side of the table that is using it will come across as being very agreeable and easy to work with.

It all starts with the negotiator that is using the give and take technique making a series of concessions to the other side. What may have seemed like significant issues that needed to be worked out before the negotiations started, quickly get resolved and often get resolved in favor of one side of the table.

As you may have guessed, this is all part of the tactic. In a sales negotiation things are never as straightforward as they may seem.

Why This Technique Works So Well

As things start to go better than expected for one side of the negotiation, a very natural thing will start to happen – they'll let their guard down. When the give and take technique is being used, breaks or pauses in the negotiations are very important to the side that is using this technique.

The reason that these breaks are so important is because of what the side that is making the unexpected progress will do during those breaks – they will tell the world about how well things are going. This could be as simple as placing a call to their management.

What has happened contains the key to why this technique works so well. The other side of the table has now become psychologically conditioned to close the deal. Since they've told the world that things are going well, they have clearly communicated that a deal is going to be reached. Now they are committed.

This is when the negotiator that is using the give and take technique can strike. You can start to take back everything that you've already given. You can do this by demanding concessions from the other side that effectively weaken or even negate the concessions that you've already made.

An example of this would be if you had agreed to sell a piece of property to the other side of the table. Let's say that you've made a big concession on the price already. In this second part of the negotiation, after the other side has already committed to making a deal, you start to turn the tables on them.

You can demand that they pay for the survey of the property. You can make them pay this year's taxes on the property. You can have them pay to move you off of this property and onto another piece of property. You can see how you can very quickly make back all of the money that you gave away up front.

What All of This Means for You

The give and take technique is a clever way to make the other side of the table give you exactly what you want. It starts out simply enough with you giving in to the other side's requests.

It's important to take breaks in order to allow the other side to communicate to the outside world that they are making progress in the negotiations. Once that's been done, the give and take negotiator can strike. Because the other side is now committed to making a deal, you can take back your concessions and get even more out of them.

It takes a great deal of planning in order to use the give and take technique. However, it is very powerful because it works over time – it's never clear just exactly what you are up to until the negotiations are almost over. They say that it's better to give than it is to receive, but in sales negotiations it's actually better to give and take!

Chapter 9

Sales Negotiators Know That a Good Bargain Can Close a Deal

Chapter 9: Sales Negotiators Know That A Good Bargain Can Close A Deal

When you are negotiating with the other side of the table, you want them to agree to your deal. In order to make this happen, you have to find a way to motivate them to "buy" what you are selling. One of the most powerful ways to make this happen is to offer them a bargain...

What Is A Bargain?

Face it, we all like bargains. Why would we behave any differently when we are in a sales negotiation? As a negotiator, you need to realize this and find ways to use it to your best advantage.

The power of a bargain is so strong that even if we aren't sure that we really need something, we'll go ahead and buy it if we think that it's a bargain. Sometimes the presence of a bargain is what it can take to close a deal.

You need to understand how bargains work on the other side. The first thing that you need to come to grips with is that a bargain is really just a state of mind. What this means is that the details of the bargain that you are offering to the other side don't really matter. What matters is what is going on in the mind of the other side of the table – do they feel as though they are being offered a bargain that they just can't pass up?

Additionally, once you understand the power of a bargain, you need to take advantage of it. This means that whatever you are offering to the other side of the table needs to be presented in such a way that they will perceive it as being offered a real bargain.

The Power of an Unused Bargain

One of the greatest types of bargains that I've been able to use in my sales negotiations is what I like to call the "unused option". It turns out that there's something that car dealers have known for a long time that we should all take the time to learn.

Car dealers make a lot of money by selling us options for our new cars that we want but really don't need. More often than not, the other side of the table will be willing to pay for options and extras that go along with what you are offering them. In fact, they'll be so highly motivated to obtain these extras that your product will look even more attractive just because you have these options. It really doesn't matter if the other side would ever actually go ahead and use these features; just having them is enough to make your product look like even more of a bargain.

What All of This Means for You

In order to get the other side of the table to commit to striking a deal with you, you've got to offer them something that they just can't refuse. One powerful way to do this is to offer them what they'll see as a clear bargain because everyone likes a bargain.

There are a number of ways to package your offer as a bargain. The key thing that you need to do is to change the other side's state of mind so that they clearly believe that they are getting a bargain. Additionally, the more options and extras that you can offer the greater the value the other side will put on what you are offering.

Taken together, these techniques provide you with a way to create an offer with a bargain that no one will be able to refuse. Take the time to find ways to turn your offer into something that the other side of the table sees as a bargain and you'll be able to close more deals and close them quicker!

Chapter 10

Why Taking Hostages During a Negotiation Is Never a Good Idea

Chapter 10: Why Taking Hostages During a Negotiation Is Never a Good Idea

We've all see what the image looks like on TV: the bad guys break-in somewhere, things go wrong, and all of a sudden they take hostages. This is never a good thing and it can very quickly go very wrong. The same thing can happen during your next business negotiation – the other side of the table may decide to take hostages — assets not people hopefully. If they do this, then how should you respond?

Why Do People Take Hostages During A Business Negotiation?

People take hostages during a business negotiation because they think that it's going to help them to get what they want out of the negotiations. Simply put, hostages are collateral that the other side thinks that they are going to be able to trade for something that they want later on in the negotiations.

In a business negotiation, a hostage can be just about anything. The list includes goods, money, trade secrets, or even something as valuable as a company's good name.

When the other side takes hostages during a negotiation, what they are trying to do is to limit the actions that you can take. Simply by them having hostages, you will find that you are unable to take actions that you normally would be able to.

How Can You React When Hostages Are Taken?

There is no way that you can really prevent the other side of the table from taking hostages during a negotiation if that's what they have their mind set to do. What that means is that you're going to have to come up with some countermeasures to use when they do it.

The first of these, and the one that seems to appeal to most male negotiators, is to consider taking some hostages of your own. Look, if they are going to do it then why shouldn't you? Remember, in the end there's going to be no difference between you and them if you take this route.

Another approach is to be willing to forfeit the hostage. Yes, just decide to let the other side keep whatever they've taken. Once you've made this decision, all of a sudden the value of the hostage immediately drops to zero for both sides. I'd like to caution you to not to expect to get the hostage back if you make this decision – the other side will never give you that satisfaction.

If you aren't comfortable with either of these approaches, then another way to deal with a hostage situation is to simply ignore it. I know that this may sound like madness, but you'd be amazed at just how effective it can turn out to be. The other side desperately wants to talk about the hostages that they've taken. If you aren't interested in having that discussion, it will end up driving them crazy.

These are all good ways to react when the other side takes hostages, but an even better thing to do is to prevent the hostages from being taken in the first place. If you want to diminish the possibility that the other side will take hostages in the first place, then you need to take the first steps.

One way to go about doing this will occur as the negotiations start. Right off the bat you can lay down some guidelines that will make it difficult for the other side to take hostages. Establish severe penalties for the taking of hostages. Your goal has to be to make sure that the other side understands that taking hostages will be an unprofitable course of action for them!

What Does All of This Mean For You

All too often during a business negotiation, hostages can be taken. There is really no way that you can prevent the other side from doing this so you had better come prepared for it to happen.

If hostages are taken, then you need to have countermeasures at the ready. Making the other side pay a steep price for their action can eliminate the value that they think that they are going to get from taking hostages in the first place. An even better approach is to take steps as the negotiations start to ensure that the other side understands that taking hostages would be an expensive mistake for them.

A good negotiator understands that taking hostages is a way for the other side to try to have more bargaining power. Realize that this can happen and always come prepared with your own set of hostage rescue techniques!

Chapter 11

To Prepare For the Future, You Need To Learn To Delight Your Customer

Chapter 11: To Prepare For the Future, You Need To Learn To Delight Your Customer

Just exactly what will it take to make your next negotiation a success? Sorry about this, but it's not going to be the negotiation styles or negotiating techniques that you use. If we keep in mind the cardinal rule of negotiating that each negotiation is just a single step along a path with the other side of the table, we need to ensure that this negotiation leads to a successful next negotiation. How are we going to make this happen?

The Power of Delight

The key to making the other side of the negotiating table leave the negotiations with a sense of satisfaction is to find ways to delight them during the negotiations. This is less of a tangible thing and much more of a feeling thing.

I'm sure that you've been delighted at some point in your life. The way that this happens is that as you are going along and something unexpected happens that makes you happy. Your happiness grows simply because this is something that you were not expecting.

This sense of "delight" is what you are going to want to cause the other side of the table to experience during your next negotiation. The true power of this is that they will remember this long after the negotiations are over and done with. Since you always have to anticipate that you'll be negotiating with this party again, this is exactly what you want them to remember!

How You Can Use Delight In Your Next Negotiation

If we can all agree that instilling a sense of delight into the other side of the table is what we want to accomplish during our next negotiation, then this all leads to the big question, how are we going to go about doing this?

The easiest way to cause delight to happen is to give something away to the other side of the table without them even having to ask for it. In the world of selling new and used cars, this is often done by including free floor mats or oil changes into the deal that is being negotiated.

Take a look at what you are negotiating and determine what you could throw in for free. At the right time in the negotiations when there is a lull and when the end of the negotiation is in view, offer it to the other side. This ensures that your offer will be both unexpected and warmly received.

What All of This Means to You

Smart negotiators know that every principled negotiation with another party may just be the first of many such negotiations. That's why it is so very important to find ways to "delight" the other side of the table – this is what they'll end up remembering about the negotiations.

The easiest way to delight the other side is to provide them with something free that they were not expecting. In order to do this, you need determine what they'd like to have and then find the right time to present them with it.

By delighting the other side of the table during your next negotiation, you'll be setting the stage for your next negotiation with them. They'll come away from this negotiation happy and pleased and when they show up next time, they'll be in the mood to reach an agreement with you quickly.

Chapter 12

The Secret Goal of Every Negotiation

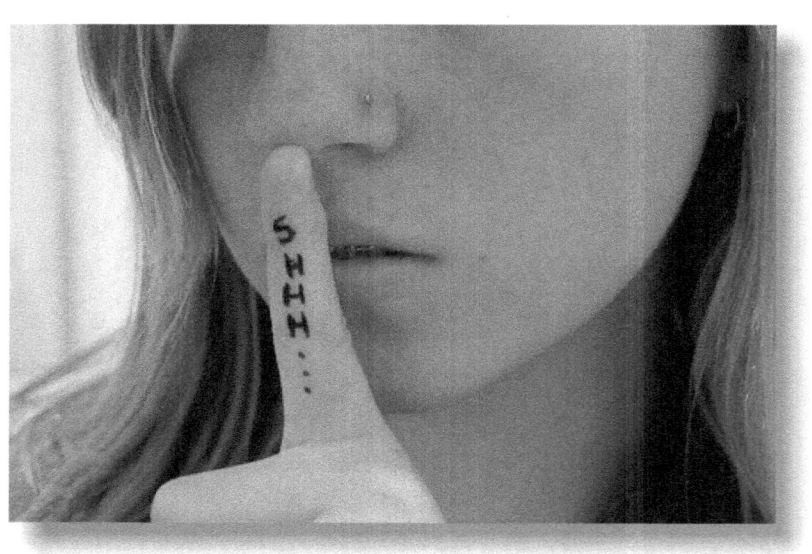

Chapter 12: The Secret Goal of Every Negotiation

Have you ever suspected that there was some set of secret negotiation styles or negotiating techniques that the really good negotiators knew that you didn't? Well, I'm going to let you know that there is one secret that you have to know if you want to be a success at negotiating. What's even better is that I am willing to share it with you and thereby make you a much better negotiator...

The Secret to Negotiating Success

What is this secret that you must know in order to be a successful negotiator you ask? Why it's very simple: in order for any negotiation to be successful, both sides of the table have to leave with a feeling of satisfaction. Yep, it's really that easy. Or is it?

All too often when I'm talking with other negotiators, most often guys, they'll tell me that when they enter into a negotiation their goal is to "win". The sad fact that I always end up sharing with them is that they are missing the point if they think that that goal is going to result in a good deal. For you see, whatever deal that you are finally able to reach with the other side needs to be one that both of you can live with. If you have "won", then the other side has "lost" and they're not going to be happy about the final deal.

One of the other key reasons that satisfaction is such a critical part of every negotiation is because this negotiation is not the end of the road. Something that can be all too easy for a negotiator to overlook is the fact that you'll probably be negotiating with the other side of the table again in the future. If you don't provide them with satisfaction this time, then they'll remember that the next time that you sit down with them and things will go badly for you.

How to Achieve Success in a Negotiation

If we can all agree that the secret to long-term negotiating success is to find ways to provide both sides of the table with satisfaction, then we can move on to the next question. Just exactly how are you expected to find ways to create this satisfaction thing?

You might think that in order to achieve satisfaction in a negotiation, one or the other sides would like to show up, win, and send the other side home a loser. However, it turns out that even if that happened, you wouldn't be happy because you'd always have that nagging feeling that perhaps you could have gotten more.

The key here is to understand that every negotiation is a compromise. There is give-and-take that goes on until both sides feel that they've gotten what they came for. If you can do this, and do it well, then you'll develop a reputation for being a fair negotiator. People will come to understand that when they negotiate with you they'll walk away feeling satisfied and so they'll be willing to spend the time negotiating with you.

What All of This Means for You

In order to be successful in the game of negotiating, you need to know what the secret to long-term success is. If you show up at a principled negotiation hoping to crush the other side of the table, then you'll quickly learn that any deals you do reach are not as good as the deals that you could have reached.

Instead, you need to learn how to create a sense of satisfaction on the parts of both sides. This is not an easy thing to do. You'll need to take the time to engage in back-and-forth discussions that allow both sides to give things up in order to get what they really want.

If you are willing to step away from the "winner takes all" mentality of negotiating and instead adopt a strategy of looking for ways to create satisfaction, then your reputation will grow. This kind of satisfaction based reputation is what is going to end up making you the negotiator that everyone wants to do a deal with.

It's from the forge of failure that the steel of success is formed.

Hard Work Does Not Guarantee Success, But Success Does Not Happen Without Hard Work.

- Dr. Jim Anderson

Create An Effective Negotiating Team At Your Company!

Dr. Jim Anderson is available to provide training and coaching on the topics that are the most important to people who have to negotiate: how can my team effectively prepare for and execute a successful negotiation that will get us what we both want and need?

Dr. Anderson believes that in order to both learn and remember what he says, audiences need to laugh. Each one of his speeches is full of fun and humor so that what he says "sticks" with everyone.

Dr. Anderson's Negotiating Training Includes:

1. How to plan for a negotiation: what information do you need and where can you find it?

2. What's the best way to explore how a deal can be created during a negotiation?

3. How can you bring a negotiation to a close without giving in to the other side?

Dr. Jim Anderson works with over 100 customers per year. To invite Dr. Anderson to work with you, contact him at:

Phone: 813-418-6970 or
Email: jim@BlueElephantConsulting.com

Speaking.   Negotiating.   Managing.   Marketing.

Photo Credits:

Cover - By: Asenat29
https://www.flickr.com/photos/72153088@N08/

Chapter 1 - By: Andy Wilson
https://www.flickr.com/photos/by_andy/

Chapter 2 – By: The Fixer
https://www.flickr.com/photos/fixersphotos/

Chapter 3 - By: Matt
https://www.flickr.com/photos/dippy_duck/

Chapter 4 - By: debbielytle
https://www.flickr.com/photos/debbiring/with/3843311508/

Chapter 5 – By: jayneandd
https://www.flickr.com/photos/jayneandd/

Chapter 6 - By: NoHoDamon
https://www.flickr.com/photos/nohodamon/

Chapter 7 – By: Cheon Fong Liew
https://www.flickr.com/photos/liewcf/

Chapter 8 – By: G Travels
https://www.flickr.com/photos/g_travels/

Chapter 9 - By: Roadside Pictures
https://www.flickr.com/photos/roadsidepictures/

Chapter 10 - By: Vook
https://www.flickr.com/photos/vooktv/

Chapter 11 - By: Mrehan
https://www.flickr.com/photos/mrehan00/

Chapter 12 - By: Val.Pearl
https://www.flickr.com/photos/valpearl/

Other Books By The Author

Product Management

- How Product Managers Can Grow Their Career: How Product Managers Can Find And Succeed In The Right Job

- Sales Secrets For Product Managers: Tips & Techniques For Product Managers To Better Understand How To Sell Their Product

- Product Management Secrets: Techniques For Product Managers To Boost Product Sales And Increase Customer Satisfaction

- Product Development Lessons For Product Managers: How Product Managers Can Create Successful Products

- Customer Lessons For Product Managers: Techniques For Product Managers To Better Understand What Their Customers Really Want

- Product Failure Lessons For Product Managers: Examples Of Products That Have Failed For Product

Managers To Learn From

- Communication Skills For Product Managers: The Communication Skills That Product Managers Need To Know How To Use In Order To Have A Successful Product

- How To Have A Successful Product Manager Career: The Things That You Need To Be Doing TODAY In Order To Have A Successful Product Manager Career

- Product Manager Product Success: How to keep your product on track and make it become a success

Public Speaking

- How To Become A Better Speaker By Changing How You Speak: Change techniques that will transform a speech into a memorable event

- How To Give A Great Presentation: Presentation techniques that will transform a speech into a memorable event

- How To Rehearse In Order To Give The Perfect Speech: How to effectively rehearse your next speech to that your message be remembered forever!

- Secrets To Creating The Perfect Speech: How to create a speech that will make your message be remembered forever!

- Secrets To Organizing The Perfect Speech: How to organize the best speech of your life!

- Secrets To Planning The Perfect Speech: How to plan to give the best speech of your life

- How To Show What You Mean During A Presentation: How to use visual techniques to transform a speech into a memorable event

CIO Skills

- How CIOs Can Solve The Security Puzzle: Tips And Techniques For CIOs To Use In Order To Secure Both Their IT Department And Their Company

- What CIOs Need To Know About Working With Partners: Techniques For CIOs To Use In Order To Be Able To Successfully Work With Partners

- Critical CIO Management Skills: Decision Making Skills That Every CIO Needs To Have In Order To Be

Able To Make The Right Choices

- How CIOs Can Make Innovation Happen: Tips And Techniques For CIOs To Use In Order To Make Innovation Happen In Their IT Department

- CIO Communication Skills Secrets: Tips And Techniques For CIOs To Use In Order To Become Better Communicators

- Managing Your CIO Career: Steps That CIOs Have To Take In Order To Have A Long And Successful Career

- CIO Business Skills: How CIOs can work effectively with the rest of the company!

IT Manager Skills

- Team Building Strategies For IT Managers: Tips And Techniques That IT Managers Can Use In Order To Develop Productive Teams

- How IT Managers Can Make Innovation Happen: Tips And Techniques For IT Managers To Use In Order To Make Innovation Happen In Their Teams

- Staffing Skills IT Managers Must Have: Tips And Techniques That IT Managers Can Use In Order To

Correctly Staff Their Teams

- Secrets Of Effective Leadership For IT Managers: Tips And Techniques That IT Managers Can Use In Order To Develop Leadership Skills

- IT Manager Career Secrets: Tips And Techniques That IT Managers Can Use In Order To Have A Successful Career

- IT Manager Budgeting Skills: How IT Managers Can Request, Manage, Use, And Track Their Funding

Negotiating

- Learn How To Signal In Your Next Negotiation: How To Develop The Skill Of Effective Signaling In A Negotiation In Order To Get The Best Possible Outcome

- Learn The Skill Of Exploring In A Negotiation: How To Develop The Skill Of Exploring What Is Possible In A Negotiation In Order To Reach The Best Possible Deal

- Learn How To Argue In Your Next Negotiation: How To Develop The Skill Of Effective Arguing In A Negotiation In Order To Get The Best Possible

Outcome

- How To Open Your Next Negotiation: How To Start A Negotiation In Order To Get The Best Possible Outcome

- Preparing For Your Next Negotiation: What You Need To Do BEFORE A Negotiation Starts In Order To Get The Best Possible Deal

How To Develop The Skill Of Assembling Potential Trades In Order To Get The Best Possible Outcome

This book has been written with one goal in mind – to show you how to successfully package trades in your next negotiation. It's not easy being a negotiator and so we're going to show you how to successfully assemble the trades that will get you the deal that you want!

Let's Make Your Negotiation A Success!

What You'll Find Inside:

- **REAL DEALS USE REAL MONEY AND SALES NEGOTIATORS NEVER FORGET IT**

- **WINNING SALES NEGOTIATIONS: THE PIZZA SECRET**

- **WHY WIN-WIN SALES NEGOTIATING NEVER WORKS AND WHAT TO DO ABOUT IT**

- **THE SECRET GOAL OF EVERY NEGOTIATION**

Dr. Jim Anderson brings his 25 years of real-world experience to this book. He's been a negotiator at some of the world's largest firms. He's going to show you what you need to do (and not do!) in order to get the best deal out of your next negotiation!

www.ingramcontent.com/pod-product-compliance
Lightning Source LLC
Chambersburg PA
CBHW071805170526
45167CB00003B/1175